HARRY POTTER POTIONS

AND MOCKTAIL COOKBOOK

30 MAGICAL DRINK RECIPES FOR MUGGLES

BY

SEBASTIAN CARPENTER

Eaglestar Books

First published by Eaglestar Books, 2020

This Continental Edition first issued by Eaglestar Books in paperback and digital edition

© Sebastian Carpenter, 2020

Printed in Great Britain

Eaglestar Books

PO Box 7086

Harrow, London

HA2 5WN, United Kingdom

CONDITIONS OF SALE:

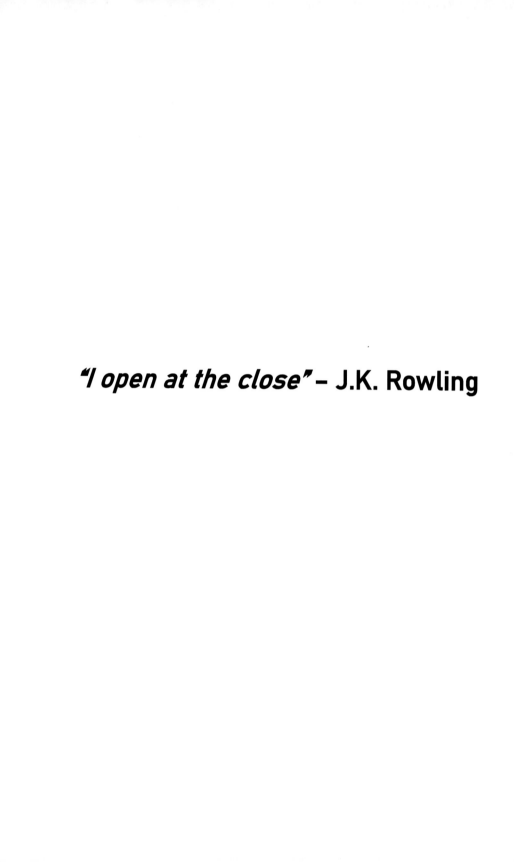

"I open at the close" – J.K. Rowling

TABLE OF CONTENTS

INTRODUCTION

J.K. Rowling is a modern English writer who authored the magical (in more ways than one!) book series about the boy wizard, *Harry Potter*. She conjured up the idea of the magical world after a delayed train journey from Manchester to London's King's Cross Station back in 1990.

A wonderful way to get involved with the wizarding world, without needing the cooking skills to follow a complicated recipe book, is by making a delicious mocktail inspired by the *Harry Potter* world.

If you're throwing a party or gathering for your witch and wizard counterparts, then this book is a must-have to set the mood for your congregation.

These simple, yet mouthwatering non-alcoholic drinks are a fantastic way of bringing a bit of The Three Broomsticks directly to your own kitchen.

Enjoy the book!

INSTRUCTIONS FOR USING THE RECIPE BOOK

Measurement Units

oz: US Fluid Ounce

1 0z. = 2 tablespoons

1 oz. = 29.57 ml

1 tablespoon = 3 teaspoons

FELIX FELICIS –

"LIQUID LUCK"

Felix Felicis or "Liquid Luck" is a potion that makes its drinker lucky for a period of time. Until the effects of the potion wear off, all of the undertakings of the guzzler tend to succeed.

"It is the colour of molten gold, and large drops leap like goldfish from its surface, never spilling."

- Harry Potter and the Half-Blood Prince,
J.K. Rowling

Preparation Time:
5 Minutes

Servings:
1

Ingredients
✓ 1 can lemon or lime soda
✓ ¼ cup of orange juice
✓ ¼ cup of lemon juice
✓ small cup
✓ 1 teaspoon. of vanilla essence and sugar
✓ food grade edible sprinkles

Instructions
1. Mix the orange juice and soda into the bowl.
2. Pour the lemon juice into the small cup with the sugar and vanilla essence.
3. Pour the lemon and vanilla mix into the bowl.
4. Add the edible sprinkles.
5. Chill and serve.

Notes
As an alternative, stir the mixture together in a saucepan over medium heat, until the liquid starts to boil and the sugar melts for a gold consistency.

DRAGON'S BLOOD PUNCH

Dragon's Blood is used in potions and other useful mixtures. It is quite expensive to purchase if it's bottled.

It has twelve listed uses, and these discoveries are mostly attributed to the esteemed headmaster of Hogwarts, Professor Dumbledore. The most notable use is as an oven cleaner.

Preparation Time:
5 Minutes

Servings:
1

Ingredients
✓ 1 can red punch (preferably Hawaiian Punch)
✓ 1 can apple juice
✓ 1 bottle cranberry juice
✓ 1 bottle ginger ale
✓ 1 cup water
✓ ice cubes

Instructions
1. Mix all of the ingredients into a large punch bowl or pot.
2. Add ice and stir.
3. Ladle into serving glasses.

PEEVES' PUMPKIN JUICE

Muggles drink orange juice, but witches and wizards grow up on pumpkin juice.

Pumpkin juice is served on the Hogwarts Express and it's widely sought after by the students of Hogwarts School of Witchcraft and Wizardry to quench their thirst.

Preparation Time:
1 hour

Servings:
2

Ingredients
- ✓ 6 cups non-alcoholic apple cider
- ✓ 15 oz. can pumpkin puree
- ✓ 1 cup apricot nectar (*or sub* peach or pear)
- ✓ 1 teaspoon. cinnamon
- ✓ ½ teaspoon. ginger
- ✓ ½ teaspoon. ground nutmeg.
- ✓ ½ cup brown sugar.

Instructions
1. Combine all ingredients into a small saucepan.
2. Bring to boil, then reduce heat and simmer for 10 to 15 minutes until pumpkin juice thickens.
3. Cool down in the refrigerator until it is ready to be served.

Notes
Can be served hot, or cold with ice. Both are equally as delicious.

GILLYWATER

Gillywater is made of Gillyweed (a magical plant) and regular water. When consumed, one develops a temporary set of gills which makes it possible to breath-in oxygen under water. It also produces webbing between your fingers and toes to aid swimming.

Professor McGonagall and Luna Lovegood both ordered Gillywater at The Three Broomsticks.

Preparation Time:
1 hour

Servings:
15

Ingredients
✓ 1 gallon water (filtered or mineral)
✓ 1 log cucumber, washed and spiralised
✓ 3 sprigs fresh mint
✓ ½ lemon juiced
✓ ice cubes

Instructions
1. Place the sliced cucumber, mint and ½ juice of lemon in a large jug.
2. Refrigerate for 1 hour.
3. Pour into glasses and serve with slices of cucumber for garnish.

Notes
The longer you infuse the combination, the stronger the flavour will become.

UNICORN'S BLOOD

Unicorn blood is said to be silver-blue and could shine under the moonlight. Firenze the centaur warned of the dangers of drinking unicorn blood:

"The blood of a unicorn will keep you alive, even if you're an inch from death, but at a terrible price. You have slain something pure and defenseless to save yourself, and you will have but a half-life, a cursed life, from the moment the blood touches your lips."

- Harry Potter and the Philosopher's Stone,
J.K. Rowling

Preparation Time:
5 Minutes

Servings:
2

Ingredients
✓ 2 cans 7up
✓ 1 teaspoon. grenadine
✓ 1 teaspoon. silver cake shimmer
✓ 1 cup of cherry Kool-Aid
✓ maraschino cherries, for garnish
✓ sprig of mint, for garnish
✓ ice cubes

Instructions
1. Place ice into a jar.
2. Add in 7up, grenadine, and cherry Kool-Aid. Stir.
3. Add in silver cake shimmer and stir.
4. Garnish with maraschino cherries and mint.

Notes
For fun, dress it up with a unicorn cocktail pick or spooky skull cocktail pick for Halloween.

BLOODY MARY BARON

The Bloody Baron is the infamous and terrifying ghost of the Slytherin House at Hogwarts.

"Harry looked over at the Slytherin table and saw a horrible ghost sitting there, with blank staring eyes, a gaunt face, and robes stained with silver blood."

- J.K. Rowling

Preparation Time:
5 Minutes

Servings:
6

Ingredients
- ✓ 36 oz. tomato juice
- ✓ juice of two lemons
- ✓ 1 teaspoon horse radish
- ✓ ½ teaspoon Worcestershire sauce
- ✓ ½ teaspoon celery salt
- ✓ ¼ kosher salt
- ✓ ¼ white pepper
- ✓ 12 dashes of hot sauce (Tabasco)
- ✓ ice cubes
- ✓ slices of lemon, for garnish
- ✓ celery sticks, for garnish

Instructions
1. Combine all the ingredients into a bowl and mix.
2. Add ice.
3. Finish the drink off with a celery sticks and a slice of lemon in each glass.

Notes
Use a highball glass for maximum effect.

SIRIUS BLACK LEMONADE

Harry Potter's Godfather, Sirius Black, may have been reckless Azkaban-escapee but he is without doubt one of the most iconic characters in the series.

Charcoal lemonade is the perfect way to stay hydrated, detox and celebrate Padfoot.

Preparation Time:
5 Minutes

Servings:
1

Ingredients
✓ juice of one lemon
✓ 1-2 capsules of activated charcoal
✓ stevia or maple syrup
✓ water
✓ ice cubes

Instructions
1. Cut lemon in half and squeeze it with juicer releasing the juice.
2. Open 1 or 2 activated charcoal capsules depending on the recommended dosage (check bottle or container).
3. Add to the lemon juice and stir to combine.
4. Fill the glass to the brim with ice and water.
5. Add in 5 drops of the stevia or maple syrup to sweeten.

Notes
It's important to consume enough water when taking activated charcoal.

DUMBLEDORE'S
SHERBET LEMON

A drink recipe inspired by Albus Dumbledore's favourite muggle sweet, lemon sherbet.

In *Harry Potter and the Chamber of Secrets*, the password for Dumbledore's office is "Lemon Drop".

Preparation Time:
5 Minutes

Servings:
1

Ingredients
✓ 1.25 oz. lemon juice
✓ ¾ oz. simple syrup
✓ 4 oz. club soda, chilled
✓ sugar
✓ ice cubes

Instructions
1. Place a small pile of sugar on a surface. Take a glass and wet the rim with a lemon. Dip the rim of the glass in the sugar, getting a good coating around the rim.
2. Mix into the shaker the ice cubes, simple syrup, and lemon juice. Shake together for 20 seconds.
3. Pour in into a glass and top it off with club soda.

Notes
Garnish with lemon peel or anything else that takes your fancy.

POLYJUICE POTION

Polyjuice Potion is one of the hardest potions to brew in the *Harry Potter* world.

The concoction enables the drinker to assume the appearance of someone else, and it can last anywhere from ten minutes to twelve hours depending on how well it has been made.

- Harry Potter and the Half-Blood Prince,
J.K. Rowling

Preparation Time:
5 Minutes

Servings:
3

Ingredients
- ✓ 3 oz. lime sherbet
- ✓ 2 cans lemon–lime soda
- ✓ 2 cans ginger ale
- ✓ green food colouring

Instructions
1. In a punch bowl, scoop in the lime sherbet.
2. Slowly pour in lemon–lime soda and ginger ale. If the drink gets too foamy, give it a stir to break up the foam.
3. Add a few drops of green food colouring.
4. Serve straight away with more lime sherbet or whipped cream on top.

Notes
Whipped cream can be added for a topping.

BUTTERBEER

Butterbeer is served at some famous locations in the wizarding world such as The Three Broomsticks, Hogsmeade and The Leaky Cauldron, Diagon Alley.

"Enjoy a foaming mug of this popular wizarding beverage."

– J.K. Rowling

Preparation Time:
20 Minutes

Servings:
4

Ingredients
- ✓ 4 bottles vanilla cream soda
- ✓ 1 tablespoon butter, softened
- ✓ ½ teaspoon cinnamon
- ✓ ¼ teaspoon nutmeg
- ✓ 7oz. marshmallow cream
- ✓ whipped cream

Instructions
1. Pour the butter, vanilla cream soda, cinnamon, and nutmeg into a bowl. Gently roll back and forth in the bowl a few times to disperse the flavours.
2. To prepare the cream topping, combine the marshmallow cream and whipped cream. Whisk until you get soft peaks.
3. To serve, place a tablespoon of topping cream in a glass, and pour the soda over the cream for a frothier topping.

Notes
As an alternative, try freezing the cream topping for 15 minutes to create a batter that can be poured over the vanilla cream soda. It will rise to the top of the glass.

FLEUR DELACOUR'S –
VEELA COLADA

Fleur Delacour is one quarter "Veela" (a fairy-like, half-human magical creature) after her father married a half-Veela witch.

Ginny Weasley gave Fleur the unpleasant nickname of "phlegm". But don't let this put you off your drinks!

Preparation Time:
5 Minutes

Servings:
3

Ingredients
- ✓ 2 cups unsweetened pineapple juice
- ✓ ¾ cup unsweetened coconut milk
- ✓ 2 tablespoons brown sugar
- ✓ ice cubes
- ✓ pineapple wedges, for garnish
- ✓ maraschino cherries, for garnish

Instructions
1. Pour the pineapple juice, coconut milk and brown sugar into a blender.
2. Add the ice cubes, enough to reach the level of the juice. Blend for 30 seconds until smooth.
3. Garnish the glasses with pineapple wedges and maraschino cherries.

Notes
Chill the glasses while blending the juice by filling them with crushed ice. Empty the crushed ice before pouring the Veela Colada.

FIREBOLT

Harry Potter received the world-class Firebolt broomstick as a gift from his godfather, Sirius Black.

The Firebolt was a costly broomstick; and it was used by the Irish and Bulgarian International Quidditch teams.

Preparation Time:
5 Minutes

Servings:
1

Ingredients
✓ 1 can or bottle of cola
✓ 1 tablespoon cherry grenadine syrup
✓ 1 tablespoon lime juice
✓ ice cubes
✓ 1 strip of lemon zest, for garnish

Instructions
1. Pour the grenadine and lime juice into a tall glass.
2. Pour in the cola to mix.
3. Add the ice cubes and float a strip of lemon juice on top to garnish.

AVADA KEDAVRA KIWI

Avada Kedavra is the Killing Curse and one of the three Unforgivable curses.

The curse manifests as a jet of green light that causes immediate, painless death. It is recognised by wizardkind as Lord Voldemort's signature curse.

Preparation Time:
5 Minutes

Servings:
1

Ingredients
✓ 3 kiwis
✓ 2 tablespoons kiwi syrup
✓ 1 can Limca
✓ ice cubes
✓ 1 lemon
✓ sugar powder
✓ mint leaves, for garnish

Instructions
1. Peel and chop kiwi. Crush ice cubes into a glass and coat the rim with sugar powder and lemon juice.
2. Pour kiwi syrup and lemon juice into glass.
3. Add chopped kiwi pieces and Limca.
4. Garnish with kiwi slice and mint leaves.

DOBBY'S DELIGHT

Dobby was a lovable male house-elf who served the Malfoy family.

He was about 3 and a half feet tall.

"Dobby is free."

Preparation Time:
5 Minutes

Servings:
1

Ingredients
√ 1 oz. 7up
√ 4 oz. lemonade
√ 1 oz. Monin Granny Smith apple syrup
√ ice cubes
√ maraschino cherries, for garnish

Instructions
1. Fill a shaker full of ice.
2. Pour 7up, lemonade and apple syrup slowly into the shaker. Stir gently.
3. Strain mixture into a serving glass.
4. Garnish the glasses maraschino cherries at the bottom of drink.

SEAMUS' IRISH COFFEE

This Irish coffee treat is dedicated to the Irish half-blood wizard, Seamus Finnigan.

Keeping with the Irish theme, Seamus' Patronus was a Banshee.

Preparation Time:
15 Minutes

Servings:
2

Ingredients
✓ 2 cups strong black coffee
✓ 2 teaspoons light brown sugar
✓ ¼ teaspoon rum extract, alcohol free
✓ ½ cup whipped cream
✓ pineapple wedges, for garnish
✓ cocoa powder, for garnish

Instructions
1. Pour freshly brewed coffee into a glass mug. Add the sugar and rum extract and stir until dissolved.
2. Beat the cream in a bowl until thick and airy.
3. Using a jug with a spout pour the cream over the back of a spoon right in the center of the mug.

Notes
Dust the cream with cocoa powder, using a stencil if desired.

MUDBLOOD MOJITO

Mudblood is an offensive word for a Muggle-born or Half-blood wizard.

It is a term used for a witch or wizard who have no wizarding family members. Draco Malfoy once called Hermione Grainger "Mudblood".

Preparation Time:
5 Minutes

Servings:
2

Ingredients
✓ 1 cup 100% pomegranate juice
✓ 1 cup sparkling white grape juice or coconut water
✓ ½ lime, juiced
✓ ice cubes
✓ pomegranate seeds, for garnish
✓ lime wedges, for garnish

Instructions
1. Mix the pomegranate juice, sparkling grape juice, and lime juice.
2. Add a small handful of pomegranate seeds to each glass.
3. Garnish with lime wedges if desired.

Notes
For flavoured ice, add ½ cup coconut water and 3 pomegranate arils to the ice tray. Freeze.

WEASLEY'S
BLACKBERRY GINGER

Ginger is a Weasley trait and there are no exceptions. Celebrate this wonderful pure-blood wizarding family with us.

"Red hair and a hand-me-down robe. You must be a Weasley."

- J.K. Rowling

Preparation Time:
5 minutes

Servings:
1

Ingredients
✓ 5 whole blackberries
✓ ½ lemon thinly sliced
✓ 1 small can ginger ale
✓ ice cubes
✓ 1 teaspoon honey

Instructions
1. Add the blackberries and lemon slices into a glass.
2. Add the ice cubes. Slowly, pour ginger ale. Add a teaspoon of honey and stir.
3. Garnish the glasses with pineapple wedges and maraschino cherries.

Notes
A straw can be used to crush the blackberries.

DIGGORY'S DAIQUIRI

Hunky Hufflepuff, Cedric Diggory, is a *Harry Potter* fan favourite.

"He's that tall, good-looking one, isn't he?"

- J.K. Rowling

Preparation Time:
5 minutes

Servings:
1

Ingredients
✓ Handful frozen strawberries, tops cut off
✓ 1 tablespoon simple syrup
✓ 4 oz. soda water
✓ ½ lime, juice only
✓ fresh mint, for garnish

Instructions
1. Place strawberries into a blender with syrup, lime juice and soda water. Blend together until you have a smooth icy paste.
2. Pour into glasses and garnish with fresh mint and garnish.

THE GOLDEN SNITCH

The Golden Snitch is a walnut-sized gold-coloured ball with silver wings.

To end the Quidditch match, the seeker has to catch the Golden Snitch.

Preparation Time:
5 minutes

Servings:
1

Ingredients
- ✓ 2 oz. cold lapsang souchong tea
- ✓ 2 oz. lemon juice
- ✓ 1 teaspoon marmalade
- ✓ 1 teaspoon honey
- ✓ ice cubes
- ✓ dried orange, thinly sliced, for garnish

Instructions
1. Put the cold tea, lemon juice and marmalade into a shaker. Stir well to break everything down and so the marmalade dissolves.
2. Stir in the honey, then add ice. Shake well.
3. Add dried orange, for garnish.

Notes
Chill the glasses in the fridge beforehand.

WOLFSBANE

The Wolfsbane Potion relives, but does not cure, the symptoms of werewolfery.

Any werewolves who consume this concoction will transform from a dangerous beast, into a sleepy wolf.

Preparation Time:
5 minutes

Servings:
1

Ingredients
- ✓ 1 can sparkling water or club soda
- ✓ ¼ cup blueberry lavender syrup
- ✓ 1 lime wedge
- ✓ ice cubes
- ✓ lime wheels, for garnish
- ✓ blueberries, for garnish

Instructions
1. Fill a tall glass with ice.
2. Add the blueberry syrup, squeeze in the lime wedge and pour the sparkling water. Gently mix.
3. Garnish the glasses with lime wheels and blueberries.

UMBRIDGE'S PERFECTLY PINK

Dolores Umbridge was a wicked woman who had a deep desire to inflict pain, and a love for all things pink.

Justice was served against her, as she was sentenced to Azkaban for crimes against Muggle-borns.

Preparation Time:
1 hour

Servings:
4

Ingredients
- ✓ 1 can frozen pink lemonade concentrate, thawed
- ✓ 4 cups white cranberry juice cocktail
- ✓ 4 cups lemon-lime soft drink, chilled
- ✓ raspberries, for garnish
- ✓ fresh citrus wedges, for garnish

Instructions
1. Pour lemonade concentrate and cranberry juice concentrate into a jug and stir well. Cover and chill for one hour.
2. After, stir in the lemon-lime soft drink.
3. Garnish the glasses with raspberries and citrus wedges.

THE GODRIC GRYFFINDOR

Godric Gryffindor was a medieval wizard and one of the four founders of Hogwarts School of Witchcraft and Wizardry.

At one point in time, the Potter family had a home in Godric's Hollow, a village in the West County of England named after Godric Gryffindor.

Preparation Time:
5 minutes

Servings:
1

Ingredients
- ✓ 3 oz. lemonade
- ✓ 6 oz. iced tea
- ✓ lemon slices, for garnish

Instructions
1. Pour the lemonade and iced tea into a glass filled with ice. Stir well.
2. Garnish the glass with lemon slices.

Notes
Try it with homemade lemonade, all you need is water, sugar and a few lemons.

HALLOWEEN HORCRUX

Halloween is a significant date in the *Harry Potter* universe as the 31st October was the date Lord Voldemort stormed Godric's Hollow and murdered the Potters.

A Horcrux is a "receptable prepared by dark magic in which a Dark Wizard has intentionally hidden a fragment of his soul for the purpose of attaining immortality."

- J.K. Rowling

Preparation Time:
5 minutes

Servings:
3

Ingredients
- ✓ 2 cups orange juice, chilled
- ✓ 1 cup tonic water, chilled
- ✓ juice of 1 lemon
- ✓ ¼ cup honey
- ✓ 1 tablespoon black non-pareils crushed, for garnish
- ✓ 2 drops red and 5 drops yellow food colouring

Instructions
1. Pour the orange juice, lemon juice and honey into a blender. Mix it thoroughly and add food colouring.
2. Crush the non-pareils onto a plate and dip the rims of the glasses into this for the cobweb look.
3. Finish by adding tonic water to the mixture and fill the glasses.

MCGONAGALL'S MANGO

Professor McGonagall is highly respected at Hogwarts and held the posts of Transfiguration teacher, head of Gryffindor House and deputy headmistress.

She is feisty and fierce, much like this mocktail.

"They're supposed to be, you blithering idiot."

– J.K. Rowling

Preparation Time:
10 minutes

Servings:
2

Ingredients
- ✓ 2 cans ginger beer
- ✓ 1 mango
- ✓ Juice of ½ lime
- ✓ ice cubes, crushed
- ✓ mango slices, for garnish
- ✓ mint, for garnish
- ✓ lime, for garnish

Instructions
1. Cut the mango into slices and put it into a blender to create a mango purée.
2. Pour the mango purée into a shaker with the ginger beer and lime juice. Stir well (don't shake!).
3. Add some crushed ices to the glasses and top it off with the mango drink. Garnish with the mango, mint and lime. dried orange, for garnish.

THE BAGSHOT BEET

This beautiful mocktail is dedicated to the magical historian and author of *A History of Magic,* a textbook used at Hogwarts School.

After Bathilda's death, Lord Voldemort re-animated her body as a hiding place for his snake Nagini.

Preparation Time:
5 minutes

Servings:
1

Ingredients
- ✓ 2 oz. beet juice
- ✓ 3/4 oz. lemon juice
- ✓ 1 can Red Bull, sugar free
- ✓ ice cubes

Instructions
1. Pour the beet juice and lemon juice into a glass filled with ice. Stir well.
2. Add the sugar free Red Bull. Mix well and serve.

Notes
Try it with rosemary for a classy garnish.

DEMENTOR'S KISS

The Dementor's Kiss was used as a punishment against criminals by the Ministry of Magic. It is a soul-sucking act that leaves the receiver in a state of despair and hopelessness.

Under Kingsley Shacklebolt, Azkaban was purged of Dementors.

Preparation Time:
5 minutes

Servings:
1

Ingredients
✓ 1 oz. grenadine
✓ 8 oz. coke
✓ 1 maraschino cherry, for garnish

Instructions
1. Pour the grenadine into a glass filled with ice. Add the coke. Stir well.
2. Garnish the glass with maraschino cherry.

GOBLET OF FIRE

The Goblet of Fire acted served as an evenhanded judge for the Triwizard Tournament by selecting a student to represent their respective school.

Harry's name was put into the Goblet of Fire by Barty Crouch Junior whilst disguised as "Mad-Eye" Moody.

Preparation Time:
10 minutes

Servings:
1

Ingredients
- ✓ 10 oz. apple cider
- ✓ 1 teaspoon pumpkin butter
- ✓ cinnamon sticks, for garnish
- ✓ Star anise, for garnish

Instructions
1. Heat the apple cider.
2. Stir in the pumpkin butter.
3. Garnish with the star anise and cinnamon sticks.

Notes
On warmer days, try the mocktail with ice.

HAGRID'S TREACLE TOFFEE

Hagrid was known for his treacle toffee and treacle fudge.

One thing Hagrid couldn't conjure, however, was a Patronus. The spell was too difficult for him to master.

Preparation Time:
5 minutes

Servings:
2

Ingredients
- ✓ ½ cup toffee nut syrup
- ✓ ¾ cup banana juice
- ✓ ¾ cup pear juice
- ✓ ½ cup apple juice
- ✓ 1 teaspoon syrup
- ✓ ice cubes
- ✓ banana slices, for garnish

Instructions
1. Combine all ingredients into shaker filled with ice cubes. Shake vigorously.
2. Pour into glasses filled with ice cubes.
3. Garnish the glass with banana slices.

RAVENCLAW'S
RHUBARB SPECIAL

Rowena Ravenclaw was one of the four founders of Hogwarts School of Witchcraft and Wizardry, as well as being considered "the most brilliant which of her time."

She also designed the everchanging floor plan and staircases at Hogwarts.

Preparation Time:
5 minutes

Servings:
2

Ingredients
✓ 1.5 oz. lime juice
✓ 1 oz. basil syrup
✓ 3 dashes rhubarb bitters
✓ ice cubes
✓ 1 bottle carbonated water
✓ rhubarb, for garnish

Instructions
1. Pour the lime juice, basil syrup and rhubarb bitters into a glass filled with ice. Stir well.
2. Top it off with the carbonated water.
3. Garnish the glass with rhubarb.

CRYSTALLISED PINEAPPLE

Crystallised Pineapple was a sweet sold at Honeydukes Sweetshop.

It is Professor Slughorn's favourite treat; and Tom Riddle may have tempted Slughorn into divulging the information he needed on Horcruxes.

Preparation Time:
5 minutes

Servings:
1

Ingredients
✓ 6 oz. pure pineapple juice
✓ 3 oz. pure orange juice
✓ 10 fresh mint leaves, for garnish
✓ ¼ thin orange slice, for garnish
✓ ice cubes
✓ sugar

Instructions
1. Pour the juices and mint leaves into a shaker filled with ice. Shake well.
2. Crush the sugar onto a plate and dip the rims of the glass into this for the sugar crust look.
3. Strain the juice into a glass and garnish the glass with orange slices.

Notes
Try it with chopped pineapple chunks and a scoop of vanilla ice cream to turn this drink into a tropical juice float.

ALSO, IN THE SERIES...

Don't miss out on the best-selling book and Part One in the series: A Harry Potter Quiz For Muggles.

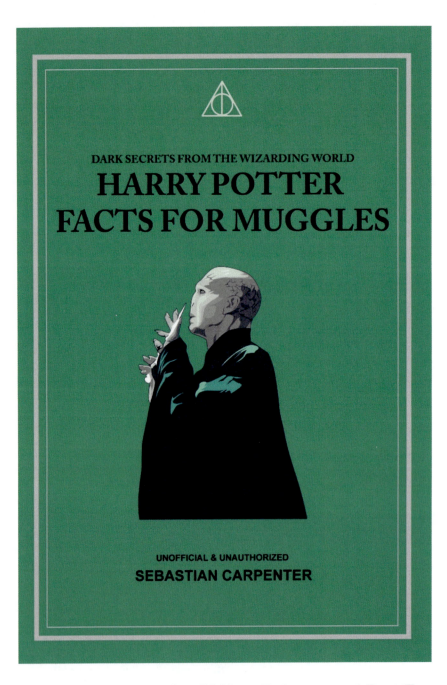

Don't miss out on the #1 New Release and Part Two in the series: Harry Potter Facts For Muggles.

ONE LAST THING

If you have enjoyed this book, please don't forget to write a **review** of this publication. It is useful feedback as well as providing untold encouragement to the author.

Made in the USA
Monee, IL
06 January 2021